"MY FIRST BAT WA COCONUT BRANC THAT DAY, ALL I WA WAS TO BE A CR

Brian Lara

IN BOOK

Cricket Annual 2022

Best Cricket Apps

Best **Cricket Apps** that Every Fan Needs in 2022

Are you looking to watch your favorite cricket Live on Mobile? Well, nowadays, most of us do not like to sit in front of the TV for the whole day. Well in my scenario, I like to pay for expensive food but always love to watch Live cricket with FREE CRICKET apps.

Now, Cricket season is almost throughout the year. Millions of fans watch cricket on live TV channels but not everyone wants to do that. Sometimes, you are in a situation where you cannot access TV i.e. in parties, clubs, work, or at college or university, agree? Then there is no better way to follow your favorite cricket match on your mobile phone or tablet than with a Best Cricket app.

Check out our article comprising a list of **10 Top Cricket Apps** for **Android** and **iPhone** to keep yourself updated regarding the live cricket match on the screen of your smartphone in case you do not have access to the TV screen or do not want to watch it on a big screen.

Here are the good cricket score apps for android and iPhone.

1# Cricbuzz – Live Cricket Scores & News

Cricbuzz is one of the most famous and widely used live score cricket app available for Android and Apple. It is very easy to use and contains numerous features like a Live Scorecard and text commentary for the ongoing live matches. Exclusive coverage of world-famous cricket leagues like IPL, PSL, BBL, and other major cricket tournaments across the world are available on cricbuzz. Cricbuzz is a free cricket app supported by ads with a clean and simple UI to navigate easily without getting lost in detail. Do download Cricbuzz app if you want a satisfactory experience with live cricket apps.

Scan the QR code and open the **Cricbuzz** on your phone or tablet.

Apple	Android

2# ESPNCricinfo

ESPNCricinfo cricket app is a well-known name for cricket enthusiasts. ESPNCricinfo made following cricket is very simple and easy through web and app. It covers every cricket tournament conducted in the cricket world. It covers live scores and ball by ball commentary, Notification updates for live cricket matches, and Cricket videos including Highlights, Analysis, Interviews, and Press conferences. ESPNCricinfo is very smooth and fast to use and loads in seconds and looks great providing visual pleasure.

Scan the QR code and open the **ESPNCricinfo** on your phone or tablet.

Apple

Android

3# NDTV Cricket App

NDTV Cricket App is one of the best **Free Cricket apps** for cricket fans. This is a complete app containing all features a cricket fan needs with a modern and clean look. This app provides the fastest live score updates via push technology with ball-by-ball commentary. You can add your favorite matches to your calendar by just tapping on the upcoming match. This is very easy to do and has no hurdles to go through. NDTV Cricket app is a free cricket app without ads but you face slow loading and minor hiccups sometimes.

Scan the QR code and open the **NDTV Cricket App** on your phone or tablet.

Apple

Android

4# The Official ICC App

The ICC Official App is one of the best apps on the list as it offers everything you need to know about the world of International cricket including fixtures, results, videos, news, team & player rankings. This app covers both men's and women's cricket offering Ball by Ball Commentary, Videos from all international Cricket events, HD Interviews, High-Quality Highlights, Breaking News, and much, much more. Sometimes, it suffers from connecting issues but overall, it is a fine live cricket app.

Scan the QR code and open the **ICC Official** on your phone or tablet.

Apple   Android

5# Yahoo Cricket App

Yahoo Cricket app is your one-stop solution to know about all information regarding cricket. It offers all basic cricket updates and one can also make his dream team in this app to enjoy fantasy cricket. Also, it provides Live Cricket Scores and Exclusive Content for all major Indian and International cricket tournaments.

Scan the QR code and open the **Yahoo Cricket** on your phone or tablet.

Apple   Android

6# Cricket Line Guru: Fast Live Line

Cricket Line Guru: Fast Live Line is one of the top free live cricket score apps with a simple and effective UI. No matter where you are, at home or at the office, all cricket information is so well organized that you can read it very easily. Install Cricket Line Guru to get Cricket Live Line, all information regarding International Cricket of Men and Women, Complete Match Scorecard, Ball by Ball Commentary, Notification of Live Matches, Upcoming Matches, and Tournament Information, Indian Premier League (IPL) and Pakistan Super League (PSL).

Scan the QR code and open the **Cricket Line Guru: Fast Live Line** on your phone or tablet.

Apple　　　　　　　　Android

7# CricHeroes Cricket Scoring App

CricHeroes started its project with a simple scorekeeping app but gradually it becomes a network now acknowledging cricketers for their talent and making them better by analyzing them. In this app, you can track random players, matches, and tournaments. You can follow the scores and can analyze the stats after the matches.

Scan the QR code and open the **CricHeroes Cricket Scoring** on your phone or tablet.

Apple　　　　　　　　Android

Cricket Annual 2022

Cricket Schedule 2022

Cricket Schedule 2022

The calendar year 2022 would be important for all the teams of ICC as it will feature a very important series. We have put a list of upcoming cricket series or tournaments in the year 2022 with detailed descriptions and information.

In some countries like India and South Asian countries, cricket is like religion and it is followed by more than one billion cricket fans. For ensuring fair tours for all teams, ICC has released FTP (Future Tour Program). It provides a framework for the respective boards to prepare their plans in advance with other nations on the basis of a pre-determined series tour Itinerary.

The below list provides a full timetable schedule for each country.

Month	Series Name	Venue
Dec 2021 - Jan 2022	Big Bash League 55 T20 matches / semi-final and final	Australia
Dec 2021 - Jan 2022	The Ashes 5 Test matches	Australia
Dec 2021 - Jan 2022	India Tour of South Africa 3 Test, 3 ODI and 4 T20 matches	South Africa
Jan - Feb 2022	Womens Ashes 2022 1 Test, 3 ODI and 3 T20 matches	Australia
Jan - Feb 2022	England Tour of West Indies 2022 5 T20, 3 Test Matches	West Indies
Jan - Feb 2022	New Zealand Tour of Australia 2022 3 ODI, 1 T20	Australia
February 2022	West Indies tour of India 2022 3 ODI and 3 T20 matches	India
February 2022	Sri Lanka Tour of Australia 2022 5 T20	Australia
Feb - Mar 2022	Sri Lanka tour of India 2022 2 Test 3 ODI Matches	India
Mar - Apr 2022	ICC Womens World Cup 2022 31 Matches	New Zealand
Mar - Apr 2022	Bangladesh Tour of South Africa 2022 3 ODI, 3 Test Matches	South Africa
June 2022	New Zealand Tour of England 2022 3 Test Matches	England
June 2022	South Africa Tour of India 2022 5 T20 Matches	India
June 2022	England Tour of Netherlands 2022 3 ODI matches	Netherlands
July 2022	India Tour of England 2022 3 ODI and 3 T20 matches	England
Jul - Sep 2022	South Africa Tour of England 2022 3 Test,3 ODI and 3 T20 matches	England
September 2022	Pakistan Tour of Afghanistan2022 3 ODI matches	Sri Lanka

Big Bash League
Cricket Schedule 2021/2022

Date	Match Details	Notes
Sun Dec 5 19:15 local | 08:15 GMT	Sydney Sixers vs Melbourne Stars, 1st T20 D/N Sydney Cricket Ground, Sydney	
Mon Dec 6 18:15 local | 08:15 GMT	Sydney Thunder vs Brisbane Heat, 2nd T20 D/N Manuka Oval, Canberra	
Tue Dec 7 19:15 local | 08:15 GMT	Melbourne Renegades vs Adelaide Strikers, 3rd T20 D/N Docklands Stadium, Melbourne	
Wed Dec 8 18:35 local | 07:35 GMT	Hobart Hurricanes vs Sydney Sixers, 4th T20 D/N TBC, TBC	
Wed Dec 8 17:10 local | 10:35 GMT	Perth Scorchers vs Brisbane Heat, 5th T20 D/N Optus Stadium, Perth	
Thu Dec 9 18:45 local | 08:15 GMT	Adelaide Strikers vs Melbourne Renegades, 6th T20 D/N Adelaide Oval, Adelaide	
Fri Dec 10 19:15 local | 08:15 GMT	Melbourne Stars vs Sydney Thunder, 7th T20 D/N Melbourne Cricket Ground, Melbourne	
Sat Dec 11 18:35 local | 07:35 GMT	Sydney Sixers vs Hobart Hurricanes, 8th T20 D/N Sydney Cricket Ground, Sydney	
Sat Dec 11 19:10 local | 08:10 GMT	Perth Scorchers vs Adelaide Strikers, 9th T20 D/N Optus Stadium, Perth	
Sun Dec 12 19:10 local | 08:10 GMT	Sydney Thunder vs Melbourne Stars, 10th T20 D/N Sydney Showground Stadium, Sydney	
Mon Dec 13 19:10 local | 08:10 GMT	Brisbane Heat vs Melbourne Renegades, 11th T20 D/N Carrara Oval, Queensland	
Tue Dec 14 18:40 local | 08:10 GMT	Hobart Hurricanes vs Perth Scorchers, 12th T2 D/N Bellerive Oval, Hobart	
Wed Dec 15 18:10 local | 07:10 GMT	Melbourne Stars vs Sydney Sixers, 13th T20 D/N Melbourne Cricket Ground, Melbourne	
Sun Dec 19 18:20 local | 10:20 GMT	Brisbane Heat vs Sydney Thunder, 14th T20 D/N Brisbane Cricket Ground, Brisbane	
Mon Dec 20 19:10 local | 08:10 GMT	Perth Scorchers vs Hobart Hurricanes, 15th T20 D/N Optus Stadium, Perth	
Tue Dec 21 19:10 local | 08:10 GMT	Sydney Sixers vs Adelaide Strikers, 16th T20 D/N Sydney Cricket Ground, Sydney	
Wed Dec 22 19:10 local | 08:10 GMT	Hobart Hurricanes vs Adelaide Strikers, 17th T20 D/N Docklands Stadium, Melbourne	

Big Bash League
Cricket Schedule 2021/2022

Date	Match Details	Notes
Thu Dec 23 18:10 local | 08:10 GMT	**Adelaide Strikers vs Brisbane Heat**, 18th T20 `D/N` Adelaide Oval, Adelaide	
Fri Dec 24 19:10 local | 08:10 GMT	**Hobart Hurricanes vs Melbourne Stars**, 19th T20 `D/N` Bellerive Oval, Hobart	
Sun Dec 26 19:10 local | 08:10 GMT	**Sydney Thunder vs Sydney Sixers**, 20th T20 `D/N` Sydney Showground Stadium, Sydney	
Sun Dec 26 18:10 local | 07:10 GMT	**Perth Scorchers vs Melbourne Renegades**, 21st T20 `D/N` Optus Stadium, Perth	
Mon Dec 27 18:20 local | 10:20 GMT	**Hobart Hurricanes vs Adelaide Strikers**, 22nd T20 `D/N` Bellerive Oval, Hobart	
Mon Dec 27 19:10 local | 08:40 GMT	**Brisbane Heat vs Melbourne Stars**, 23rd T20 `D/N` Brisbane Cricket Ground, Brisbane	
Tue Dec 28 18:40 local | 08:40 GMT	**Sydney Thunder vs Perth Scorchers**, 24th T20 `D/N` Manuka Oval, Canberra	
Wed Dec 29 19:40 local | 08:40 GMT	**Sydney Sixers vs Brisbane Heat**, 25th T20 `D/N` Sydney Cricket Ground, Sydney	
Wed Dec 29 19:40 local | 08:40 GMT	**Melbourne Renegades vs Hobart Hurricanes**, 26th T20 `D/N` Docklands Stadium, Melbourne	
Thu Dec 30 14:40 local | 05:10 GMT	**Perth Scorchers vs Melbourne Stars**, 27th T20 Optus Stadium, Perth	
Fri Dec 31 19:20 local | 08:20 GMT	**Adelaide Strikers vs Sydney Thunder**, 28th T20 `D/N` Adelaide Oval, Adelaide	
Sat Jan 1 16:00 local | 05:00 GMT	**Hobart Hurricanes vs Brisbane Heat**, 29th T20 Bellerive Oval, Hobart	
Sat Jan 1 19:40 local | 08:40 GMT	**Sydney Sixers vs Melbourne Renegades**, 30th T20 `D/N` TBC, TBC	
Sun Jan 2 19:10 local | 08:40 GMT	**Melbourne Stars vs Perth Scorchers**, 31st T20 `D/N` Junction Oval, Melbourne	
Sun Jan 2 19:40 local | 08:40 GMT	**Sydney Thunder vs Adelaide Strikers**, 32nd T20 `D/N` Sydney Showground Stadium, Sydney	
Mon Jan 3 18:10 local | 07:10 GMT	**Melbourne Stars vs Melbourne Renegades**, 33rd T20 `D/N` Melbourne Cricket Ground, Melbourne	
Tue Jan 4 18:20 local | 10:20 GMT	**Brisbane Heat vs Sydney Sixers**, 34th T20 `D/N` Carrara Oval, Queensland	

Big Bash League
Cricket Schedule 2021/2022

Date	Match Details	Notes
Wed Jan 5 19:40 local | 08:40 GMT	**Adelaide Strikers vs Hobart Hurricanes**, 35th T20 D/N Adelaide Oval, Adelaide	
Wed Jan 5 19:40 local | 08:40 GMT	**Perth Scorchers vs Sydney Thunder**, 36th T20 D/N Optus Stadium, Perth	
Thu Jan 6 19:40 local | 08:40 GMT	**Melbourne Renegades vs Brisbane Heat**, 37th T20 D/N Simonds Stadium, Geelong	
Thu Jan 6 16:40 local | 08:40 GMT	**Perth Scorchers vs Sydney Sixers**, 38th T20 Optus Stadium, Perth	
Fri Jan 7 16:10 local | 05:10 GMT	**Adelaide Strikers vs Melbourne Stars**, 39th T20 Adelaide Oval, Adelaide	
Sat Jan 8 18:20 local | 08:20 GMT	**Melbourne Renegades vs Sydney Thunder**, 40th T20 D/N Docklands Stadium, Melbourne	
Sat Jan 8 16:40 local | 08:40 GMT	**Brisbane Heat vs Hobart Hurricanes**, 41st T20 Brisbane Cricket Ground, Brisbane	
Sun Jan 9 19:10 local | 08:40 GMT	**Sydney Sixers vs Perth Scorchers**, 42nd T20 D/N TBC, TBC	
Mon Jan 10 16:00 local | 05:30 GMT	**Melbourne Stars vs Adelaide Strikers**, 43rd T20 Melbourne Cricket Ground, Melbourne	
Mon Jan 10 19:15 local | 08:15 GMT	**Hobart Hurricanes vs Sydney Thunder**, 44th T20 D/N TBC, TBC	
Tue Jan 11 19:15 local | 08:15 GMT	**Melbourne Renegades vs Sydney Sixers**, 45th T20 D/N Simonds Stadium, Geelong	
Wed Jan 12 19:15 local | 08:15 GMT	**Brisbane Heat vs Adelaide Strikers**, 46th T20 D/N Brisbane Cricket Ground, Brisbane	
Thu Jan 13 14:00 local | 05:00 GMT	**Sydney Thunder vs Hobart Hurricanes**, 47th T20 Sydney Showground Stadium, Sydney	
Fri Jan 14 19:45 local | 08:45 GMT	**Adelaide Strikers vs Perth Scorchers**, 49th T20 Adelaide Oval, Adelaide	
Sat Jan 15 19:45 local | 08:45 GMT	**Sydney Sixers vs Sydney Thunder**, 50th T20 Sydney Cricket Ground, Sydney	
Sun Jan 16 19:45 local | 08:45 GMT	**Melbourne Stars vs Brisbane Heat**, 51st T20 Melbourne Cricket Ground, Melbourne	
Mon Jan 17 19:45 local | 08:45 GMT	**Hobart Hurricanes vs Melbourne Renegades**, 52nd T20 Bellerive Oval, Hobart	

Big Bash League
Cricket Schedule 2021/2022

Date	Match Details	Notes
Tue Jan 18 19:45 local | 08:45 GMT	**Adelaide Strikers vs Sydney Sixers**, 53rd T20 Adelaide Oval, Adelaide	
Wed Jan 19 12:30 local | 02:30 GMT	**Brisbane Heat vs Perth Scorchers**, 54th T20 Brisbane Cricket Ground, Brisbane	
Wed Jan 19 16:40 local | 05:40 GMT	**Sydney Thunder vs Melbourne Renegades**, 55th T20 Sydney Showground Stadium, Sydney	
Wed Jan 19 19:45 local | 08:45 GMT	**Melbourne Stars vs Hobart Hurricanes**, 56th T20 Melbourne Cricket Ground, Melbourne	
Fri Jan 21 19:30 local | 08:30 GMT	**TBC vs TBC**, Eliminator T20 TBC, TBC	
Sat Jan 22 19:30 local | 08:30 GMT	**TBC vs TBC**, Qualifier T20 TBC, TBC	
Sun Jan 23 19:30 local | 08:30 GMT	**TBC vs TBC**, Knockout T20 TBC, TBC	
Wed Jan 26 19:30 local | 08:30 GMT	**TBC vs TBC**, Challenger T20 TBC, TBC	
Fri Jan 28 19:30 local | 08:30 GMT	**TBC VS TBC**, FINAL T20 TBC, TBC	

Notes

The Ashes
Cricket Schedule 2021/2022

Date	Match Details	Notes
Wed Dec 8 - Sun Dec 12 10:00 local | 12:00 GMT	**Australia vs England,** 1st Test Brisbane Cricket Ground, Brisbane	
Thu Dec 16 - Mon Dec 20 12:30 local | 02:30 GMT	**Australia vs England,** 2nd Test Adelaide Oval, Adelaide	
Sun Dec 26 - Thu Dec 30 10:30 local | 23:30 GMT	**Australia vs England,** 3rd Test Melbourne Cricket Ground, Melbourne	
Wed Jan 5 - Sun Jan 9 10:30 local | 23:30 GMT	**Australia vs England,** 4th Test Sydney Cricket Ground, Sydney	
Fri Jan 14 - Tue Jan 18 12:30 local | 02:30 GMT	**Australia vs England,** 5th Test Optus Stadium, Perth	

India Tour of South Africa
Cricket Schedule 2022

Date	Match Details	Notes
Fri Dec 17 - Tue Dec 21 10:00 local | 08:00 GMT	**South Africa vs India,** 1st Test The Wanderers Stadium, Johannesburg	
Sun Dec 26 - Thu Dec 30 10:00 local | 08:00 GMT	**South Africa vs India,** 2nd Test SuperSport Park, Centurion	
Mon Jan 3 - Fri Jan 7 10:00 local | 08:00 GMT	**South Africa vs India,** 3rd Test Newlands, Cape Town	
Tue Jan 11 10:30 local | 08:30 GMT	**South Africa vs India,** 1st ODI Boland Park, Paarl	
Fri Jan 14 10:30 local | 08:30 GMT	**South Africa vs India,** 2nd ODI Newlands, Cape Town	
Sun Jan 16 10:30 local | 08:30 GMT	**South Africa vs India,** 3rd ODI Newlands, Cape Town	
Wed Jan 19 16:00 local | 14:00 GMT	**South Africa vs India,** 1st T20 D/N Newlands, Cape Town	
Fri Jan 21 16:00 local | 14:00 GMT	**South Africa vs India,** 2nd T20 D/N Newlands, Cape Town	

India Tour of South Africa
Schedule 2022

Date	Match Details	Notes
Sun Jan 23 16:00 local | 14:00 GMT	**South Africa vs India**, 3rd T20 D/N Boland Park, Paarl	
Wed Jan 26 16:00 local | 14:00 GMT	**South Africa vs India**, 4th T20 D/N Boland Park, Paarl	

Women's Ashes
Cricket Schedule 2022

Date	Match Details	Notes
Thu Jan 27 – Mon Jan 31 10:00 local | 23:00 GMT (prev day)	**Australia Women vs England Women**, Only Test Manuka Oval, Canberra	
Fri Feb 4 19:10 local | 08:10 GMT	**Australia Women vs England Women**, 1st T20 D/N North Sydney Oval, Sydney	
Sun Feb 6 21:10 local | 08:10 GMT	**Australia Women vs England Women**, 2nd T20 D/N North Sydney Oval, Sydney	
Thu Feb 10 19:10 local | 08:10 GMT	**Australia Women vs England Women**, 3rd T20 D/N Adelaide Oval, Adelaide	
Sun Feb 13 10:05 local | 23:05 GMT	**Australia Women vs England Women**, 1st ODI Adelaide Oval, Adelaide	
Wed Feb 16 10:05 local | 23:05 GMT	**Australia Women vs England Women**, 2nd ODI Junction Oval, Melbourne	
Sat Feb 19 10:05 local | 23:05 GMT	**Australia Women vs England Women**, 3rd ODI Junction Oval, Melbourne	

Notes

England Tour of West Indies
Cricket Schedule 2022

Date	Match Details	Notes
Fri Jan 28	**West Indies vs England**, 1st T20 Kensington Oval, Bridgetown	
Sun Jan 30	**West Indies vs England**, 2nd T20 Manuka Oval, Canberra	
Wed Feb 2	**West Indies vs England**, 3rd T20 Kensington Oval, Bridgetown	
Fri Feb 4	**West Indies vs England**, 4th T20 Kensington Oval, Bridgetown	
Sat Feb 5	**West Indies vs England**, 5th T20 Kensington Oval, Bridgetown	
Tue Mar 8 - Sat Mar 12	**West Indies vs England**, 1st Test Sir Vivian Richards Stadium, Antigua	
Wed Mar 16 Sun Mar 20	**West Indies vs England**, 2nd Test Kensington Oval, Bridgetown	
Thu Mar 24 Mon Mar 28	**West Indies vs England**, 3rd Test National Cricket Stadium, St Georges	

New Zealand Tour of Australia
Cricket Schedule 2021/2022

Date	Match Details	Notes
Sun Jan 30 11:40 local | 03:40 GMT	**Australia vs New Zealand**, 1st ODI Optus Stadium, Perth	
Wed Feb 2 14:10 local | 03:10 GMT	**Australia vs New Zealand**, 2nd ODI D/N Bellerive Oval, Hobart	
Sat Feb 5 14:10 local | 03:10 GMT	**Australia vs New Zealand**, 3rd ODI D/N Sydney Cricket Ground, Sydney	
Tue Feb 8 19:10 local | 08:10 GMT	**Australia vs New Zealand**, Only T20 Manuka Oval, Canberra	

West Indies tour of India
Cricket Schedule 2022

Date	Match Details	Notes
Sun Feb 6 13:30 local | 08:00 GMT	**India vs West Indies**, 1st ODI **D/N** Sardar Patel Stadium Motera, Ahmedabad	
Wed Feb 9 13:30 local | 08:00 GMT	**India vs West Indies**, 2nd ODI **D/N** Sawai Mansingh Stadium, Jaipur	
Sat Feb 12 13:30 local | 08:00 GMT	**India vs West Indies**, 3rd ODI **D/N** Eden Gardens, Kolkata	
Tue Feb 15 19:00 local | 13:30 GMT	**India vs West Indies**, 1st T20 **D/N** Barabati Stadium, CuttackDr. Y S Rajasekhara Reddy ACA-VDCA Cricket Stadium, Visakhapatnam	
Sun Feb 20 19:00 local | 13:30 GMT	**India vs West Indies**, 3rd T20 **D/N** Greenfield International Stadium, Thiruvananthapuram	

Sri Lanka Tour of Australia
Cricket Schedule 2022

Date	Match Details	Notes
Fri Feb 11 19:00 local | 08:00 GMT	**Australia vs Sri Lanka**, 1st T20 **D/N** Sydney Cricket Ground, Sydney	
Sun Feb 13 18:10 local | 08:10 GMT	**Australia vs Sri Lanka**, 2nd T20 **D/N** Brisbane Cricket Ground, Brisbane	
Tue Feb 15 18:10 local | 08:10 GMT	**Australia vs Sri Lanka**, 3rd T20 **D/N** Carrara Oval, Queensland	
Fri Feb 18 18:10 local | 08:10 GMT	**Australia vs Sri Lanka**, 4th T20 **D/N** Adelaide Oval, Adelaide	
Sun Feb 20 15:30 local | 04:30 GMT	**Australia vs Sri Lanka**, 5th T20 **D/N** Melbourne Cricket Ground, Melbourne	

Sri Lanka tour of India
Cricket Schedule 2022

Date	Match Details	Notes
Fri Feb 25 – Tue Mar 1 09:30 local | 04:00 GMT	**India vs Sri Lanka,** 1st Test M.Chinnaswamy Stadium, Bangalore	
Sat Mar 5 – Wed Mar 9 09:30 local | 04:00 GMT	**India vs Sri Lanka,** 2nd Test Punjab C.A. Stadium, Mohali	
Sun Mar 13 19:00 local | 13:30 GMT	**India vs Sri Lanka,** 1st T20 D/N Punjab C.A. Stadium, Mohali	
Tue Mar 15 19:00 local | 13:30 GMT	**India vs Sri Lanka,** 2nd T20 D/N HPCA Stadium, Dharamsala	
Fri Mar 18 19:00 local | 13:30 GMT	**India vs Sri Lanka,** 3rd T20 D/N Atal Bihari Vajpayee Stadium, Lucknow	

ICC Women's World Cup
Cricket Schedule 2022

Date	Match Details	Notes
Fri Mar 4 14:00 local | 01:00 GMT	**New Zealand Women vs TBC,** 1st ODI Bay Oval, Mt Maunganui	
Sat Mar 5 10:00 local | 21:00 GMT	**TBC vs South Africa Women,** 2nd OD University Oval, Dunedin	
Sat Mar 5 14:00 local | 01:00 GMT	**Australia Women vs England Women,** 3rd ODI Seddon Park, Hamilton	
Sun Mar 6 14:00 local | 01:00 GMT	**TBC vs India Women,** 4th ODI D/N Bay Oval, Mt Maunganui	
Mon Mar 7 10:00 local | 21:00 GMT	**New Zealand Women vs TBC,** 5th ODI D/N University Oval, Dunedin	
Tue Mar 8 14:00 local | 01:00 GMT	**Australia Women vs TBC,** 6th ODI Bay Oval, Mt Maunganui	
Wed Mar 9 10:00 local | 21:00 GMT	**TBC vs England Women,** 7th ODI D/N University Oval, Dunedin	
Thu Mar 10 14:00 local | 01:00 GMT	**New Zealand Women vs India Women,** 8th ODI D/N Seddon Park, Hamilton	

ICC Women's World Cup
Cricket Schedule 2022

Date	Match Details	Notes
Fri Mar 11 14:00 local | 01:00 GMT	**TBC vs South Africa Women**, 9th ODI Bay Oval, Mt Maunganui	
Sat Mar 12 14:00 local | 01:00 GMT	**TBC vs India Women**, 10th ODI **D/N** Seddon Park, Hamilton	
Sun Mar 13 10:00 local | 21:00 GMT	**New Zealand Women vs Australia Women**, 11th ODI Basin Reserve, Wellington	
Mon Mar 14 10:00 local | 21:00 GMT	**TBC vs TBC**, 12th ODI Seddon Park, Hamilton	
Mon Mar 14 14:00 local | 01:00 GMT	**South Africa Women vs England Women**, 13th ODI Bay Oval, Mt Maunganui	
Tue Mar 15 10:00 local | 21:00 GMT	**Australia Women vs TBC**, 14th OD Basin Reserve, Wellington	
Wed Mar 16 14:00 local | 01:00 GMT	**England Women vs India Women**, 15th ODI **D/N** Bay Oval, Mt Maunganui	
Thu Mar 17 14:00 local | 01:00 GMT	**New Zealand Women vs South Africa Women**, 16th ODI **D/N** Seddon Park, Hamilton	
Fri Mar 18 10:00 local | 21:00 GMT	**TBC vs TBC**, 17th ODI **D/N** Bay Oval, Mt Maunganui	
Sat Mar 19 14:00 local | 01:00 GMT	**India Women vs Australia Women**, 18th ODI **D/N** Eden Park, Auckland	
Sun Mar 20 10:00 local | 21:00 GMT	**New Zealand Women vs England Women**, 19th ODI Eden Park, Auckland	
Mon Mar 21 14:00 local | 01:00 GMT	**TBC vs TBC**, 20th ODI Seddon Park, Hamilton	
Tue Mar 22 10:00 local | 21:00 GMT	**South Africa Women vs Australia Women**, 21st OD Basin Reserve, Wellington	
Tue Mar 22 14:00 local | 01:00 GMT	**India Women vs TBC**, 22nd ODI Seddon Park, Hamilton	
Thu Mar 24 10:00 local | 21:00 GMT	**South Africa Women vs TBC**, 23rd ODI Basin Reserve, Wellington	
Thu Mar 24 14:00 local | 01:00 GMT	**England Women vs TBC**, 24th ODI Hagley Oval, Christchurch	
Fri Mar 25 10:00 local | 21:00 GMT	**TBC vs Australia Women**, 25th ODI Basin Reserve, Wellington	

ICC Women's World Cup
Cricket Schedule 2022

Date	Match Details	Notes
Sat Mar 26 10:00 local | 21:00 GMT	**New Zealand Women vs TBC**, 26th ODI Hagley Oval, Christchurch	
Sun Mar 27 10:00 local | 21:00 GMT	**England Women vs TBC**, 27th ODI Basin Reserve, Wellington	
Sun Mar 27 14:00 local | 01:00 GMT	**India Women vs South Africa Women**, 28th ODI D/N Hagley Oval, Christchurch	
Wed Mar 30 10:00 local | 21:00 GMT	**TBC vs TBC**, 1st Semi Final ODI Basin Reserve, Wellington	
Thu Mar 31 14:00 local | 01:00 GMT	**TBC vs TBC**, 2nd Semi Final ODI Hagley Oval, Christchurch	
Sun Apr 3 14:00 local | 01:00 GMT	**TBC vs TBC**, Final ODI Hagley Oval, Christchurch	

Bangladesh Tour of South Africa
Cricket Schedule 2022

Date	Match Details	Notes
Fri Mar 18 13:30 local | 08:00 GMT	**South Africa vs Bangladesh**, 1st ODI TBC, TBC	
Sun Mar 20 13:30 local | 08:00 GMT	**South Africa vs Bangladesh**, 2nd ODI D/N TBC, TBC	
Wed Mar 23 13:30 local | 08:00 GMT	**South Africa vs Bangladesh**, 3rd ODI D/N TBC, TBC	
Wed Mar 30 - Sun Apr 3 11:00 local | 05:30 GMT	**South Africa vs Bangladesh**, 1st Test TBC, TBC	
Thu Apr 7 - Mon Apr 11 11:00 local | 05:30 GMT	**South Africa vs Bangladesh**, 2nd Test TBC, TBC	

New Zealand Tour of England
Schedule 2022

Date	Match Details	Notes
Thu Jun 2 - Mon Jun 6 11:00 local | 10:00 GMT	**England vs New Zealand**, 1st Test Lords, London	
Fri Jun 10 - Tue Jun 14 11:00 local | 10:00 GMT	**England vs New Zealand**, 2nd Test Trent Bridge, Nottingham	
Thu Jun 23 - Mon Jun 27 11:00 local | 10:00 GMT	**England vs New Zealand**, 3rd Test Headingley, Leeds	

South Africa Tour of India
Schedule 2022

Date	Match Details	Notes
Thu Jun 9 19:00 local | 13:30 GMT	**India vs South Africa**, 1st T20 D/N MA Chidambaram Stadium - Chepauk, Chennai	
Sun Jun 12 19:00 local | 13:30 GMT	**India vs South Africa**, 2nd T20 D/N M.Chinnaswamy Stadium, Bangalore	
Tue Jun 14 19:00 local | 13:30 GMT	**India vs South Africa**, 3rd T20 D/N Vidarbha Cricket Association Stadium, Nagpur	
Wed Jun 15 19:00 local | 13:30 GMT	**India vs South Africa**, 4th T20 D/N Saurashtra Cricket Association Stadium, Rajkot	
Sun Jun 19 19:00 local | 13:30 GMT	**India vs South Africa**, 5th T20 D/N Feroz Shah Kotla, Delhi	

Notes

England Tour of Netherlands
Schedule 2022

Date	Match Details	Notes
Fri Jun 17 10:30 local | 08:30 GMT	**Netherlands vs England**, 1st ODI VRA Cricket Ground, Amstelveen	
Sun Jun 19 10:30 local | 08:30 GMT	**Netherlands vs England**, 2nd ODI VRA Cricket Ground, Amstelveen	
Wed Jun 22 10:30 local | 08:30 GMT	**Netherlands vs England**, 3rd ODI VRA Cricket Ground, Amstelveen	

India Tour of England
Schedule 2022

Date	Match Details	Notes
Fri Jul 1 18:30 local | 17:30 GMT	**England vs India**, 1st T20 `D/N` Old Trafford, Manchester	
Sun Jul 3 14:30 local | 13:30 GMT	**England vs India**, 2nd T20 Trent Bridge, Nottingham	
Wed Jul 6 18:30 local | 17:30 GMT	**England vs India**, 3rd T20 `D/N` The Rose Bowl, Southampton	
Sat Jul 9 11:00 local | 10:00 GMT	**England vs India**, 1st ODI Edgbaston, Birmingham	
Tue Jul 12 13:00 local | 12:00 GMT	**England vs India**, 2nd ODI `D/N` Kennington Oval, London	

Notes

South Africa Tour of England
Cricket Schedule 2022

Date	Match Details	Notes
Tue Jul 19 13:00 local | 12:00 GMT	**England vs South Africa,** 1st ODI D/N Melbourne Cricket Ground, Melbourne	
Fri Jul 22 13:00 local | 13:00 GMT	**England vs South Africa,** 2nd ODI Old Trafford, Manchester	
Sun Jul 24 11:00 local | 10:00 GMT	**England vs South Africa,** 3rd ODI Headingley, Leeds	
Wed Jul 27 18:30 local | 17:30 GMT	**England vs South Africa,** 1st T20 D/N County Ground, Bristol	
Thu Jul 28 18:30 local | 17:30 GMT	**England vs South Africa,** 2nd T20 D/N Sophia Gardens, Cardiff	
Sun Jul 31 14:30 local | 13:30 GMT	**England vs South Africa,** 3rd T20 D/N The Rose Bowl, Southampton	
Wed Aug 17 – Sun Aug 21 11:00 local | 10:00 GMT	**England vs South Africa,** 1st Test Lords, London	
Thu Aug 25 – Mon Aug 29 11:00 local | 10:00 GMT	**England vs South Africa,** 2nd Test Edgbaston, Birmingham	
Thu Sep 8 – Mon Sep 12 11:00 local | 10:00 GMT	**England vs South Africa,** 3rd Test Kennington Oval, London	

Pakistan Tour of Afghanistan
Schedule 2022

Date	Match Details	Notes
Thu Sep 1 10:45 local | 09:45 GMT	**Afghanistan vs Pakistan,** 1st ODI Mahinda Rajapaksa International Stadium, Hambantota	
Sat Sep 3 10:45 local | 09:45 GMT	**Afghanistan vs Pakistan,** 2nd ODI Mahinda Rajapaksa International Stadium, Hambantota	
Mon Sep 5 10:45 local | 09:45 GMT	**Afghanistan vs Pakistan,** 3rd ODI Mahinda Rajapaksa International Stadium, Hambantota	

Bookie details

Bookie Details

Username

Bookie

Password

Email

Notes

Username

Bookie

Password

Email

Notes

Username

Bookie

Password

Email

Notes

Bookie Details

Username

Bookie

Password

Email

Notes

Username

Bookie

Password

Email

Notes

Username

Bookie

Password

Email

Notes

Cricket Annual 2022

Daily Betting

Date				
Time				
Selection				
Course				
Odds				
The bet				
Stake				
Return				
LOSS				
PROFIT				

Date				
Time				
Selection				
Course				
Odds				
The bet				
Stake				
Return				
LOSS				
PROFIT				

Date				
Time				
Selection				
Course				
Odds				
The bet				
Stake				
Return				
LOSS				
PROFIT				

Date				
Time				
Selection				
Course				
Odds				
The bet				
Stake				
Return				
LOSS				
PROFIT				

Date				
Time				
Selection				
Course				
Odds				
The bet				
Stake				
Return				
LOSS				
PROFIT				

Date				
Time				
Selection				
Course				
Odds				
The bet				
Stake				
Return				
LOSS				
PROFIT				

Date				
Time				
Selection				
Course				
Odds				
The bet				
Stake				
Return				
LOSS				
PROFIT				

Date				
Time				
Selection				
Course				
Odds				
The bet				
Stake				
Return				
LOSS				
PROFIT				

Date				
Time				
Selection				
Course				
Odds				
The bet				
Stake				
Return				
LOSS				
PROFIT				

Date				
Time				
Selection				
Course				
Odds				
The bet				
Stake				
Return				
LOSS				
PROFIT				

Date				
Time				
Selection				
Course				
Odds				
The bet				
Stake				
Return				
LOSS				
PROFIT				

Date				
Time				
Selection				
Course				
Odds				
The bet				
Stake				
Return				
LOSS				
PROFIT				

Date				
Time				
Selection				
Course				
Odds				
The bet				
Stake				
Return				
LOSS				
PROFIT				

Date				
Time				
Selection				
Course				
Odds				
The bet				
Stake				
Return				
LOSS				
PROFIT				

Date				
Time				
Selection				
Course				
Odds				
The bet				
Stake				
Return				
LOSS				
PROFIT				

Date				
Time				
Selection				
Course				
Odds				
The bet				
Stake				
Return				
LOSS				
PROFIT				

Date				
Time				
Selection				
Course				
Odds				
The bet				
Stake				
Return				
LOSS				
PROFIT				

Date				
Time				
Selection				
Course				
Odds				
The bet				
Stake				
Return				
LOSS				
PROFIT				

Date				
Time				
Selection				
Course				
Odds				
The bet				
Stake				
Return				
LOSS				
PROFIT				

Date				
Time				
Selection				
Course				
Odds				
The bet				
Stake				
Return				
LOSS				
PROFIT				

Date				
Time				
Selection				
Course				
Odds				
The bet				
Stake				
Return				
LOSS				
PROFIT				

Date				
Time				
Selection				
Course				
Odds				
The bet				
Stake				
Return				
LOSS				
PROFIT				

Date				
Time				
Selection				
Course				
Odds				
The bet				
Stake				
Return				
LOSS				
PROFIT				

Date				
Time				
Selection				
Course				
Odds				
The bet				
Stake				
Return				
LOSS				
PROFIT				

Date				
Time				
Selection				
Course				
Odds				
The bet				
Stake				
Return				
LOSS				
PROFIT				

Date				
Time				
Selection				
Course				
Odds				
The bet				
Stake				
Return				
LOSS				
PROFIT				

Date				
Time				
Selection				
Course				
Odds				
The bet				
Stake				
Return				
LOSS				
PROFIT				

Date				
Time				
Selection				
Course				
Odds				
The bet				
Stake				
Return				
LOSS				
PROFIT				

Date				
Time				
Selection				
Course				
Odds				
The bet				
Stake				
Return				
LOSS				
PROFIT				

Date				
Time				
Selection				
Course				
Odds				
The bet				
Stake				
Return				
LOSS				
PROFIT				

Date				
Time				
Selection				
Course				
Odds				
The bet				
Stake				
Return				
LOSS				
PROFIT				

Date				
Time				
Selection				
Course				
Odds				
The bet				
Stake				
Return				
LOSS				
PROFIT				

Date				
Time				
Selection				
Course				
Odds				
The bet				
Stake				
Return				
LOSS				
PROFIT				

Date				
Time				
Selection				
Course				
Odds				
The bet				
Stake				
Return				
LOSS				
PROFIT				

Date				
Time				
Selection				
Course				
Odds				
The bet				
Stake				
Return				
LOSS				
PROFIT				

Date				
Time				
Selection				
Course				
Odds				
The bet				
Stake				
Return				
LOSS				
PROFIT				

Date				
Time				
Selection				
Course				
Odds				
The bet				
Stake				
Return				
LOSS				
PROFIT				

Date				
Time				
Selection				
Course				
Odds				
The bet				
Stake				
Return				
LOSS				
PROFIT				

Date				
Time				
Selection				
Course				
Odds				
The bet				
Stake				
Return				
LOSS				
PROFIT				

Date				
Time				
Selection				
Course				
Odds				
The bet				
Stake				
Return				
LOSS				
PROFIT				

Date				
Time				
Selection				
Course				
Odds				
The bet				
Stake				
Return				
LOSS				
PROFIT				

Date				
Time				
Selection				
Course				
Odds				
The bet				
Stake				
Return				
LOSS				
PROFIT				

Date				
Time				
Selection				
Course				
Odds				
The bet				
Stake				
Return				
LOSS				
PROFIT				

Date				
Time				
Selection				
Course				
Odds				
The bet				
Stake				
Return				
LOSS				
PROFIT				

Date				
Time				
Selection				
Course				
Odds				
The bet				
Stake				
Return				
LOSS				
PROFIT				

Date				
Time				
Selection				
Course				
Odds				
The bet				
Stake				
Return				
LOSS				
PROFIT				

Date				
Time				
Selection				
Course				
Odds				
The bet				
Stake				
Return				
LOSS				
PROFIT				

Date				
Time				
Selection				
Course				
Odds				
The bet				
Stake				
Return				
LOSS				
PROFIT				

Date				
Time				
Selection				
Course				
Odds				
The bet				
Stake				
Return				
LOSS				
PROFIT				

Date				
Time				
Selection				
Course				
Odds				
The bet				
Stake				
Return				
LOSS				
PROFIT				

Date				
Time				
Selection				
Course				
Odds				
The bet				
Stake				
Return				
LOSS				
PROFIT				

Date				
Time				
Selection				
Course				
Odds				
The bet				
Stake				
Return				
LOSS				
PROFIT				

Date				
Time				
Selection				
Course				
Odds				
The bet				
Stake				
Return				
LOSS				
PROFIT				

Date				
Time				
Selection				
Course				
Odds				
The bet				
Stake				
Return				
LOSS				
PROFIT				

Date				
Time				
Selection				
Course				
Odds				
The bet				
Stake				
Return				
LOSS				
PROFIT				

Date				
Time				
Selection				
Course				
Odds				
The bet				
Stake				
Return				
LOSS				
PROFIT				

Date				
Time				
Selection				
Course				
Odds				
The bet				
Stake				
Return				
LOSS				
PROFIT				

Date				
Time				
Selection				
Course				
Odds				
The bet				
Stake				
Return				
LOSS				
PROFIT				

Date				
Time				
Selection				
Course				
Odds				
The bet				
Stake				
Return				
LOSS				
PROFIT				

Date				
Time				
Selection				
Course				
Odds				
The bet				
Stake				
Return				
LOSS				
PROFIT				

Date				
Time				
Selection				
Course				
Odds				
The bet				
Stake				
Return				
LOSS				
PROFIT				

Date				
Time				
Selection				
Course				
Odds				
The bet				
Stake				
Return				
LOSS				
PROFIT				

Date				
Time				
Selection				
Course				
Odds				
The bet				
Stake				
Return				
LOSS				
PROFIT				

Date				
Time				
Selection				
Course				
Odds				
The bet				
Stake				
Return				
LOSS				
PROFIT				

Date				
Time				
Selection				
Course				
Odds				
The bet				
Stake				
Return				
LOSS				
PROFIT				

Date				
Time				
Selection				
Course				
Odds				
The bet				
Stake				
Return				
LOSS				
PROFIT				

Date				
Time				
Selection				
Course				
Odds				
The bet				
Stake				
Return				
LOSS				
PROFIT				

Date				
Time				
Selection				
Course				
Odds				
The bet				
Stake				
Return				
LOSS				
PROFIT				

Date				
Time				
Selection				
Course				
Odds				
The bet				
Stake				
Return				
LOSS				
PROFIT				

Date				
Time				
Selection				
Course				
Odds				
The bet				
Stake				
Return				
LOSS				
PROFIT				

Date				
Time				
Selection				
Course				
Odds				
The bet				
Stake				
Return				
LOSS				
PROFIT				

Date				
Time				
Selection				
Course				
Odds				
The bet				
Stake				
Return				
LOSS				
PROFIT				

Date				
Time				
Selection				
Course				
Odds				
The bet				
Stake				
Return				
LOSS				
PROFIT				

Date				
Time				
Selection				
Course				
Odds				
The bet				
Stake				
Return				
LOSS				
PROFIT				

Date				
Time				
Selection				
Course				
Odds				
The bet				
Stake				
Return				
LOSS				
PROFIT				

Date				
Time				
Selection				
Course				
Odds				
The bet				
Stake				
Return				
LOSS				
PROFIT				

Date				
Time				
Selection				
Course				
Odds				
The bet				
Stake				
Return				
LOSS				
PROFIT				

Date				
Time				
Selection				
Course				
Odds				
The bet				
Stake				
Return				
LOSS				
PROFIT				

Date				
Time				
Selection				
Course				
Odds				
The bet				
Stake				
Return				
LOSS				
PROFIT				

Date				
Time				
Selection				
Course				
Odds				
The bet				
Stake				
Return				
LOSS				
PROFIT				

Date				
Time				
Selection				
Course				
Odds				
The bet				
Stake				
Return				
LOSS				
PROFIT				

Date				
Time				
Selection				
Course				
Odds				
The bet				
Stake				
Return				
LOSS				
PROFIT				

Date				
Time				
Selection				
Course				
Odds				
The bet				
Stake				
Return				
LOSS				
PROFIT				

Date				
Time				
Selection				
Course				
Odds				
The bet				
Stake				
Return				
LOSS				
PROFIT				

Date				
Time				
Selection				
Course				
Odds				
The bet				
Stake				
Return				
LOSS				
PROFIT				

Date				
Time				
Selection				
Course				
Odds				
The bet				
Stake				
Return				
LOSS				
PROFIT				

Date				
Time				
Selection				
Course				
Odds				
The bet				
Stake				
Return				
LOSS				
PROFIT				

Date				
Time				
Selection				
Course				
Odds				
The bet				
Stake				
Return				
LOSS				
PROFIT				

Date				
Time				
Selection				
Course				
Odds				
The bet				
Stake				
Return				
LOSS				
PROFIT				

Date				
Time				
Selection				
Course				
Odds				
The bet				
Stake				
Return				
LOSS				
PROFIT				

Date				
Time				
Selection				
Course				
Odds				
The bet				
Stake				
Return				
LOSS				
PROFIT				

Date				
Time				
Selection				
Course				
Odds				
The bet				
Stake				
Return				
LOSS				
PROFIT				

Date				
Time				
Selection				
Course				
Odds				
The bet				
Stake				
Return				
LOSS				
PROFIT				

Date				
Time				
Selection				
Course				
Odds				
The bet				
Stake				
Return				
LOSS				
PROFIT				

Date				
Time				
Selection				
Course				
Odds				
The bet				
Stake				
Return				
LOSS				
PROFIT				

Date				
Time				
Selection				
Course				
Odds				
The bet				
Stake				
Return				
LOSS				
PROFIT				

Date				
Time				
Selection				
Course				
Odds				
The bet				
Stake				
Return				
LOSS				
PROFIT				

Date				
Time				
Selection				
Course				
Odds				
The bet				
Stake				
Return				
LOSS				
PROFIT				

Date				
Time				
Selection				
Course				
Odds				
The bet				
Stake				
Return				
LOSS				
PROFIT				

Date				
Time				
Selection				
Course				
Odds				
The bet				
Stake				
Return				
LOSS				
PROFIT				

Date				
Time				
Selection				
Course				
Odds				
The bet				
Stake				
Return				
LOSS				
PROFIT				

Date				
Time				
Selection				
Course				
Odds				
The bet				
Stake				
Return				
LOSS				
PROFIT				

Date				
Time				
Selection				
Course				
Odds				
The bet				
Stake				
Return				
LOSS				
PROFIT				

Date				
Time				
Selection				
Course				
Odds				
The bet				
Stake				
Return				
LOSS				
PROFIT				

Date				
Time				
Selection				
Course				
Odds				
The bet				
Stake				
Return				
LOSS				
PROFIT				

Date				
Time				
Selection				
Course				
Odds				
The bet				
Stake				
Return				
LOSS				
PROFIT				

Date				
Time				
Selection				
Course				
Odds				
The bet				
Stake				
Return				
LOSS				
PROFIT				

Date				
Time				
Selection				
Course				
Odds				
The bet				
Stake				
Return				
LOSS				
PROFIT				

Date				
Time				
Selection				
Course				
Odds				
The bet				
Stake				
Return				
LOSS				
PROFIT				

Date				
Time				
Selection				
Course				
Odds				
The bet				
Stake				
Return				
LOSS				
PROFIT				

Date				
Time				
Selection				
Course				
Odds				
The bet				
Stake				
Return				
LOSS				
PROFIT				

Date				
Time				
Selection				
Course				
Odds				
The bet				
Stake				
Return				
LOSS				
PROFIT				

Date				
Time				
Selection				
Course				
Odds				
The bet				
Stake				
Return				
LOSS				
PROFIT				

Date				
Time				
Selection				
Course				
Odds				
The bet				
Stake				
Return				
LOSS				
PROFIT				

Cricket Annual 2022

Weekly betting

Weekly dates to and from

	Stakes	Loss	Profit
1 week			
2 week			
3 week			
4 week			
5 week			
6 week			
7 week			
8 week			
9 week			
10 week			
11 week			
12 week			
13 week			
14 week			
15 week			
16 week			
17 week			
18 week			
19 week			
20 week			
21 week			
22 week			
23 week			
24 week			
25 week			
26week			

Weekly dates to and from

	Stakes	Loss	Profit
27 week			
28 week			
29 week			
30 week			
31 week			
32 week			
33 week			
34 week			
35 week			
36 week			
37 week			
38 week			
39 week			
40 week			
41 week			
42 week			
43 week			
44 week			
45 week			
46 week			
47 week			
48 week			
49 week			
50 week			
51 week			
52 week			

Cricket Annual 2022

Monthly betting results

Cricket Annual 2022

Monthly Records

	Stakes	Loss	Profit
January			
February			
March			
April			
May			
June			
July			
August			
September			
October			
November			
December			

Notes

Cricket Annual 2022

Yearly review

Cricket Annual 2022

Yearly Review

Total staked	Total won	Total lost	Total profit/loss

Most profitable Day

Biggest Losing Day

Most profitable Month

Biggest Losing Month

Most satisfying bet

Worst bet placed

Biggest highlight

Biggest disappointment

Most successful bet strategy

Notes

2022 Calendar

JANUARY
2022

SUN	MON	TUE	WED	THU	FRI	SAT
						1
2	3	4	5	6	7	8
9	10	11	12	13	14	15
16	17	18	19	20	21	22
23	24	25	26	27	28	29
30	31					

FEBRUARY
2022

SUN	MON	TUE	WED	THU	FRI	SAT
		1	2	3	4	5
6	7	8	9	10	11	12
13	14	15	16	17	18	19
20	21	22	23	24	25	26
27	28					

MARCH
2022

SUN	MON	TUE	WED	THU	FRI	SAT
		1	2	3	4	5
6	7	8	9	10	11	12
13	14	15	16	17	18	19
20	21	22	23	24	25	26
27	28	29	30	31		

APRIL
2022

SUN	MON	TUE	WED	THU	FRI	SAT
					1	2
3	4	5	6	7	8	9
10	11	12	13	14	15	16
17	18	19	20	21	22	23
24	25	26	27	28	29	30

MAY
2022

SUN	MON	TUE	WED	THU	FRI	SAT
1	2	3	4	5	6	7
8	9	10	11	12	13	14
15	16	17	18	19	20	21
22	23	24	25	26	27	28
29	30	31				

JUNE
2022

SUN	MON	TUE	WED	THU	FRI	SAT
			1	2	3	4
5	6	7	8	9	10	11
12	13	14	15	16	17	18
19	20	21	22	23	24	25
26	27	28	29	30		

JULY
2022

SUN	MON	TUE	WED	THU	FRI	SAT
					1	2
3	4	5	6	7	8	9
10	11	12	13	14	15	16
17	18	19	20	21	22	23
24	25	26	27	28	29	30
31						

AUGUST
2022

SUN	MON	TUE	WED	THU	FRI	SAT
	1	2	3	4	5	6
7	8	9	10	11	12	13
14	15	16	17	18	19	20
21	22	23	24	25	26	27
28	29	30	31			

SEPTEMBER
2022

SUN	MON	TUE	WED	THU	FRI	SAT
				1	2	3
4	5	6	7	8	9	10
11	12	13	14	15	16	17
18	19	20	21	22	23	24
25	26	27	28	29	30	

OCTOBER
2022

SUN	MON	TUE	WED	THU	FRI	SAT
						1
2	3	4	5	6	7	8
9	10	11	12	13	14	15
16	17	18	19	20	21	22
23	24	25	26	27	28	29
30	31					

NOVEMBER
2022

SUN	MON	TUE	WED	THU	FRI	SAT
		1	2	3	4	5
6	7	8	9	10	11	12
13	14	15	16	17	18	19
20	21	22	23	24	25	26
27	28	29	30			

DECEMBER
2022

SUN	MON	TUE	WED	THU	FRI	SAT
				1	2	3
4	5	6	7	8	9	10
11	12	13	14	15	16	17
18	19	20	21	22	23	24
25	26	27	28	29	30	31

Cricket Annual 2022

Notes

Dear

I would appreciate it if you would leave a comment
and rate our book on Amazon. You can also add a
photo which we highly encourage :)

Tom Smith and friends ❤

Printed in Great Britain
by Amazon